BLOOM

Olympiad ACE

A Comprehensive Practice Book

for School Olympiads & Talent Search Exams

ENGLISH

Class 1

by

Srishti Agarwal

Olympiad ACE

BLOOM

Bloom Cap Edu Ventures Pvt. Ltd.

Administrative & Production Office

'Ramchhaya' 4577/15, Agarwal Road, Darya Ganj, New Delhi -110002
Tele: 011- 47630600, 43518550

PRICE: ₹125.00

Published by Arihant Publications (I) Ltd.

For further information about the books log on to
www.bloomcap.org

Follow us on

Preface

"Future belongs to those Who prepares for it today"

School Olympiads are National & International level competitions conducted by different Government, Non-Government & Educational Organisations with the purpose of making the children ready to face competitive exams.

The challenging Questions asked in Olympiads motivate them to learn more & more and bring out the best results with improved academic performance. The Awards & Scholarship offered by Olympiads motivate children to aspire & strive for doing better and emerge out to be the best.

English Olympiads

English is one of the most widely spoken languages across the world. In today's era, good command over English is considered as a must have skill. The greatest advantage of studying English is improvement in communication skills along with the growth of personality.

English Olympiads are meant to strengthen students' command over this universal language by improving spellings, grammar, sentence structure and to master student's language skills.

'Bloom English Olympiad Study Book Class 1' is a perfect resource to Study & Practice for Olympiad Exams and other National & State Level Talent Search Exams & Other Competitions.

Some Special Features of Bloom English Olympiad Study Books are;

- Complete coverage of all the aspects of English; Grammar, Reading Comprehension, Writing Skills, Spellings, Vocabulary & Communication Skills.
- Chapterwise Exercises having different types of Objective Questions at par with the Olympiad Level.
- Olympiad Pattern Practice Sets at the end.

This book is prepared by Expert Panel with the utmost care, still if you have any suggestions regarding its improvement then feel free to contact us at support@bloomcap.org. We will try to inculcate your suggestions in the further editions.

Contents

Chapter 01

Nouns

Directions (Q. Nos. 1-8) Choose the nouns from the options given below.

1. (a) Dr. Arora (b) Teaching (c) Managerial (d) Batting
2. (a) Catch (b) See (c) London (d) Hold
3. (a) Watch (b) Play (c) Boys (d) Sweet
4. (a) Fast (b) Hospital (c) Slow (d) Walking
5. (a) Army (b) Fat (c) Have (d) Short
6. (a) Simple (b) Throw (c) Fleet (d) Read
7. (a) Greatly (b) Shock (c) Ugly (d) Pretty
8. (a) Honesty (b) She (c) Happy (d) Him

Directions (Q. Nos. 9-11) State whether the following nouns are names of person, place, animal or thing.

9. Tiger
(a) Person (b) Animal (c) Place (d) Thing
10. Mother
(a) Person (b) Animal (c) Place (d) Thing
11. Television
(a) Person (b) Animal (c) Place (d) Thing

Directions (Q. Nos. 12-14) Read the sentences given below and select the noun from the given options.

12. The tea is very hot.
(a) tea (b) is (c) very (d) hot
13. Rama started shouting loudly.
(a) Rama (b) shouting (c) started (d) loudly
14. Chess is a difficult game.
(a) Chess (b) difficult (c) game (d) Both (a) and (c)
15. Choose the countable noun from the following.
(a) Stars (b) Water (c) Book (d) Sand
16. Choose the uncountable noun from the following.
(a) Curry (b) Chair (c) Page (d) Pencil

Directions (Q.Nos. 17-20) Identify the type of nouns underlined in the given sentences.

17. I like to eat jam with bread.
(a) Countable noun
(b) Uncountable noun
(c) Proper noun
(d) Abstract noun

18. I have three pens.
(a) Proper noun
(b) Collective noun
(c) Uncountable noun
(d) Countable noun

19. India is a big country.
(a) Proper noun
(b) Abstract noun
(c) Common noun
(d) Collective noun

20. Do you want to drink milk?
(a) Common noun
(b) Abstract noun
(c) Uncountable noun
(d) Collective noun

Directions (Q. Nos. 21-22) Read the passages given below and answer the questions.

21. Roby is a gaint elephant. He lives in the Sundarban jungle. He has many elephant friends. Jim is his best friend. They like to play under the Peepal tree.

How many proper nouns are there in the passage given above?

(a) 6 (b) 3 (c) 4 (d) 2

22. There are many houses in my village. But it has only one school. All the boys and girls go there to study. There are many teachers. Children enjoy studying and playing together.

How many common nouns are there in the passage given above?

(a) 5 (b) 7 (c) 4 (d) 3

Directions : (Q.Nos. 23-24) Fill in the blanks with correct nouns.

23. I do not like to eat ....
(a) jacket (b) pen
(c) chair (d) brinjal

24. A farmer lives in a ....
(a) India (b) America
(c) village (d) school

Directions (Q.Nos. 25 and 26) Choose the correct noun for the given pictures.

25.

(a) Planet (b) Earth
(c) Sun (d) Moon

26.

(a) Bouquet (b) flower
(c) Plants (d) Forest

Chapter 02

Pronouns

Directions (Q.Nos. 1-10) Identify the pronouns from the given options.

1. (a) Sahil (b) Book (c) It (d) Pen
2. (a) Paper (b) Pen (c) Mouse (d) They
3. (a) Bag (b) We (c) School (d) Table
4. (a) Chair (b) Bottle (c) He (d) Computer
5. (a) She (b) Car (c) Ball (d) Girl
6. (a) Woman (b) I (c) Leaf (d) Bench
7. (a) You (b) Boat (c) Home (d) Draw
8. (a) Colours (b) It (c) Eraser (d) Chair
9. (a) Fruit (b) Bed (c) They (d) Box
10. (a) Brush (b) Cook (c) Bake (d) We

Directions (Q. Nos. 11-15) Identify the pronoun in the sentences.

11. He is a lawyer in the High Court.
(a) He
(b) is
(c) lawyer
(d) High Court

12. Rakhi lost her money in the bus. She was very sad.
(a) She
(b) lost
(c) bus
(d) money

13. We have a big bungalow in the village. It is red in colour.
(a) We
(b) It
(c) house
(d) Both (a) and (b)

14. When will they arrive at the airport.
(a) When (b) will
(c) they (d) airport

15. You must not play with fire.
(a) You (b) must not
(c) play (d) fire

Directions (Q. Nos. 16-20) Choose the correct pronouns from the options given below to fill in the blanks.

16. Rahul is going to the book fair. .... likes to read.

(a) She (b) He
(c) It (d) You

17. The tea is cold. We cannot drink ....

(a) she (b) it
(c) we (d) he

18. Mrs Shah is my favourite teacher. .... teaches Mathematics.

(a) We (b) He
(c) She (d) They

19. You should talk to the railway authorities. .... will help you.

(a) It (b) They
(c) She (d) He

20. It is raining heavily. .... can take my umbrella.

(a) You (b) His
(c) It (d) I

21. Read the passage given below and answer the question.

Zac and Sam went to the store because they wanted food. Zac wanted burger. Sam wanted french fries. "I want to get a burger," Zac said. "I do not want to get a burger," Sam said. "I want to get french fries." "What are we going to do?" Sam asked.

How many pronouns are there in the above lines?

(a) 6 (b) 3 (c) 5 (d) 4

22. Match the sentences in List-I with the correct noun in List-II.

List I	List II
A. They are going to the market.	1. Mouse
B. He is running very fast.	2. Teena and Meena
C. It ate the cheese.	3. Lata
D. She sings beautifully.	4. Rahul

Codes

	A	B	C	D		A	B	C	D
(a)	2	3	1	4	(b)	2	4	1	3
(c)	1	4	2	3	(d)	3	2	4	1

Directions (Q. Nos. 23-27) Replace the underlined words with a pronoun.

23. Karan is an intelligent boy.

(a) It (b) He
(c) She (d) We

24. The children are studying.

(a) They (b) She
(c) We (d) He

25. Pinki is in the hospital. Pinki is not well.

(a) It (b) He
(c) You (d) She

26. Jim and his sister are playing badminton.

(a) They (b) He
(c) We (d) It

27. The theatre is houseful.

(a) She (b) It
(c) They (d) Them

Chapter 03

Verbs

Directions (1-5) Choose the verbs from the given options.

1. (a) House (b) Have
   (c) Jar (d) She

2. (a) Clean (b) Simple
   (c) Phone (d) Bangle

3. (a) Sorry (b) Speak
   (c) Couch (d) Three

4. (a) Number (b) Lesson
   (c) Pick (d) Crayons

5. (a) Story (b) Classes
   (c) They (d) Study

Directions (Q.Nos. 6-10) Choose the correct action word for the following pictures.

6. 

   (a) Sing
   (b) Drink
   (c) Bend
   (d) Swing

7. 

   (a) Draw (b) Sleep
   (c) Work (d) Eat

8. 

   (a) Jogging (b) Hopping
   (c) Skipping (d) Cycling

9. 

   (a) Riding (b) Seeing
   (c) Watching (d) Driving

10. 

    (a) Colour (b) Paint
    (c) Climb (d) Hit

Directions (Q. Nos. 11-13) Fill in the blanks with suitable verbs.

11. Jimmy .... riding a bicycle.
(a) are (b) were
(c) is (d) am

12. The joke made everyone .... loudly.
(a) leave (b) laugh
(c) jump (d) munch

13. Will you .... football with me?
(a) play (b) joy
(c) skip (d) walk

Directions (Q. Nos. 14-16) Identify the verb in the sentences.

14. Reema studies in the library.
(a) Reema (b) studies
(c) in the (d) library

15. The tailor is stitching the clothes carefully.
(a) The tailor
(b) is
(c) stitching
(d) Both (b) and (c)

16. He went home without informing anyone.
(a) He (b) went
(c) home (d) anyone

17. Match the following pictures with their verbs.

List-I	List-II
A. 	1. Singing
B. 	2. Dancing
C. 	3. Swimming
D. 	4. Writing

Codes

	A	B	C	D		A	B	C	D
(a)	1	2	3	4	(b)	4	1	2	3
(c)	2	3	4	1	(d)	3	4	1	2

Directions (Q. Nos. 18-21) Fill the blanks to complete the passage.

Ricky is ...**(18)**... to the zoo. He packs food and water in his bag. He ...**(19)**... a bicycle and parks it in the parking. He ...**(20)**... a ticket and enters the zoo.

Inside the zoo he sees the elephant is lifting its trunk. The monkeys ...**(21)**... jumping on the trees. The tiger is sleeping in his cage. The ducks are jumping in the pond.

18. (a) jogging (b) going
(c) jumping (d) walking

19. (a) drives (b) climbs
(c) rides (d) sits

20. (a) buys (b) throws
(c) sells (d) pulls

21. (a) was (b) is (c) are (d) an

Chapter 04

Adjectives

Directions (Q. Nos. 1-5) Which of the following words is an adjective?

1. Study, Proud, Neatly, Quickly

(a) Study (b) Proud
(c) Neatly (d) Quickly

2. Sight, Careless, Group, Honesty

(a) Sight (b) Careless
(c) Group (d) Honesty

3. Zone, Meeting, Chubby, Eatery

(a) Chubby (b) Zone
(c) Meeting (d) Eatery

4. Goal, Strike, Dream, White

(a) Dream (b) Strike
(c) White (d) Goal

5. Mean, Struggle, You, Belong

(a) Struggle (b) You
(c) Belong (d) Mean

Directions (Q. Nos. 6-10) Fill in the blanks with suitable adjectives.

6. The teacher gave me a .... book.

(a) ugly (b) three
(c) shiny (d) red

7. I got a .... video game on my birthday.

(a) new (b) old
(c) young (d) hard

8. The Sun is very ....

(a) cool (b) hot
(c) soft (d) fire

9. Kashmir has .... valleys.

(a) deep (b) coloured
(c) beautiful (d) high

10. My mother bought a .... pot for me.

(a) single (b) many
(c) hot (d) colourful

Directions (Q. Nos. 11-15) Find the adjectives from the given sentences. Choose the correct answer from the options given below.

11. The boy played with his green kite.

(a) boy (b) played
(c) his (d) green

12. The wet dog was playing in the water.

(a) dog (b) wet
(c) playing (d) in

13. We saw the funny clown play the guitar.

(a) guitar (b) clown
(c) funny (d) play

14. The pond for the animals is clean.

(a) clean
(b) animals
(c) for
(d) the

15. The red apple had a big worm inside.

(a) red, worm (b) big, apple
(c) red , big (d) inside

Directions (Q. Nos. 16-19) Look at the pictures and fill in the blanks using suitable adjectives.

16. Hunny bunny was too .... to reach the apple.

(a) big (b) short
(c) ride (d) long

17. I used a hand lens to see the .... ant.

(a) kind (b) short
(c) little (d) same

18. The fancy peacock spread his .... feathers.

(a) wide (b) lazy
(c) clear (d) torn

19. Jumbo the elephant is very ....

(a) hard
(b) swift
(c) small
(d) large

20. Read the passage and find the number of adjectives used in it.

We must keep our city clean and green. It is a bad habit to throw garbage on the streets. One should be a good citizen and stop littering. It is our duty to prevent our city from getting dirty.

(a) 4 (b) 6
(c) 5 (d) 3

21. Match the following adjectives in List I with suitable nouns in List II.

	List I		List II
A.	Pretty	1.	fruits
B.	Bad	2.	girl
C.	Fresh	3.	dish
D.	Tasty	4.	odour

Codes

	A	B	C	D
(a)	2	4	1	3
(b)	4	2	1	3
(c)	4	2	3	1
(d)	2	3	1	4

Chapter

05

Articles

Directions (Q. Nos. 1-8) Look at the pictures and choose suitable articles that will be used before them.

1.

(a) A (b) An
(c) The (d) None of these

2.

(a) A (b) An
(c) The (d) None of these

3.

(a) A (b) An
(c) The (d) None of these

4.

(a) A (b) An
(c) The (d) None of these

5.

(a) A
(b) An
(c) The
(d) None of these

6.

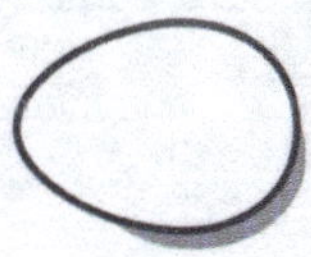

(a) A (b) An
(c) The (d) None of these

7.

(a) A (b) An
(c) The (d) None of these

8.

(a) A
(b) An
(c) The
(d) None of these

Directions (Q. Nos. 9-13) Fill in the blanks with suitable articles from options given below.

9. Batman is .... interesting movie.
(a) a (b) an
(c) the (d) None of these

10. I went to .... park yesterday.
(a) a (b) an
(c) the (d) None of these

11. Rajat saw .... owl sitting on the tree.
(a) a (b) an
(c) the (d) None of these

12. My mother baked .... cake for me.
(a) a
(b) an
(c) the
(d) None of the above

13. May I have .... glass of milk please?
(a) a
(b) an
(c) the
(d) None of the above

Directions (Q. Nos. 14-16) Read the sentences given below and choose the incorrect option.

14. (a) My father gifted me a watch on my birthday.
(b) The hen laid an egg.
(c) The teacher will come back in an hour.
(d) I visited a Taj Mahal last month.

15. (a) Mahima is an good dancer.
(b) Can I have a piece of cake?
(c) Put the sheets in a folder.
(d) I read an article in the newspaper.

16. (a) My grandmother stitched a sweater.
(b) A Ganga is a holy river.
(c) There is a park near the temple.
(d) Timy saw an octopus.

Directions (Q. Nos. 17 and 18) Read the following sentences and choose the correct option.

17. (a) My friend wants to be an pilot.
(b) She is an nice girl.
(c) This is a lovely dress.
(d) The cat is on an tree.

18. (a) Give me an pencil.
(b) I eat an apple everyday.
(c) She has a idea.
(d) My mother is the good cook.

19. Match the following.

List I	List II
I. A	A. Ambulance
II. The	B. Book
III. An	C. Red fort

Codes

	I	II	III		I	II	III
(a)	A	B	C	(b)	B	C	A
(c)	B	A	C	(d)	C	A	B

Chapter 06

Prepositions

Directions (Q. Nos. 1-8) Fill the blanks with suitable prepositions from the options given below.

1. 

The boy is .... the table.

(a) on (b) under
(c) in (d) over

2. 

The cat is sitting .... the jar.

(a) in (b) behind
(c) on (d) infront of

3. 

The mouse is .... the box.

(a) in (b) above
(c) on (d) over

4. 

A cat is sitting .... Rahul and Rohini.

(a) in (b) on
(c) between (d) by

5. 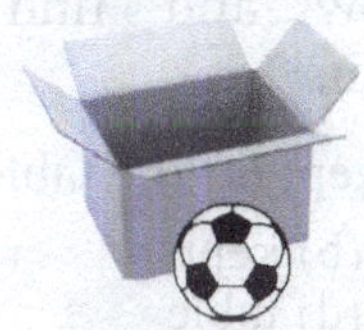

The football is kept .... the box.

(a) over (b) near (c) in (d) above

6. 

The family is travelling .... car.

(a) on (b) to (c) by (d) at

7. 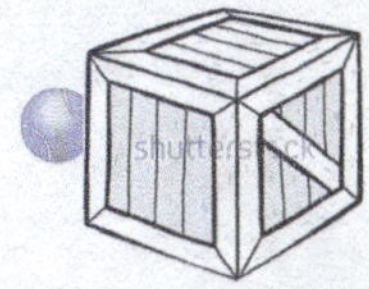

The ball is .... the chest.

(a) in (b) near (c) next (d) behind

8. 

The ball is lying .... the chest.

(a) near (b) on (c) at (d) in

Directions (Q. Nos. 9-11) Fill the blanks with the correct prepositions.

9. The students are studying .... the class.

(a) on (b) in
(c) between (d) above

10. The Sun rises .... the East.

(a) on (b) at (c) in (d) inside

11. Radha's house is .... the temple.

(a) above (b) near
(c) at (d) between

Directions (Q. Nos. 12-14) Read the sentences given below and find the preposition used in them.

12. The flower vase is kept on the table.

(a) flower vase (b) kept
(c) on (d) table

13. The girl is standing near the tree.

(a) The girl (b) near
(c) tree (d) standing

14. The hunter is looking at the deer.

(a) The hunter (b) is
(c) looking (d) at

Directions (Q. Nos. 15-16) Read the sentences given below and choose the correct option.

15. (a) Karan is sitting on the garden.
(b) Karan is sitting in the garden.
(c) Karan is sitting into the garden.
(d) Karan is sitting over the garden.

16. (a) Please keep the jar on the table.
(b) Please keep the jar in the table.
(c) Please keep the jar under the table.
(d) Please keep the jar behind the table.

Directions (Q. Nos. 17-18) Look at the picture given below and fill the blanks to complete the passage from the given options.

This is my room. I keep my room neat and tidy. My bed is placed. ...**(17)**... the windows. The computer and the lamp are kept ...**(18)**... the study table.

17. (a) behind (b) outside
(c) near (d) before

18. (a) in (b) on
(c) infront of (d) over

Chapter 07

Singular and Plural

Directions (Q. Nos. 1-8) Read the words given below and identify their plural form from the given options.

1. Child
(a) Childs (b) Children
(c) Childrens (d) None of these

2. Party
(a) Parties (b) Partys
(c) Party (d) Parteis

3. Leaf
(a) Leafs (b) Leave
(c) Leaves (d) None of these

4. Box
(a) Boxes (b) Boxs
(c) Boxies (d) Boxen

5. Woman
(a) Womans (b) Womens
(c) Women (d) None of these

6. Key
(a) Keyes (b) Keys
(c) Key (d) None of these

7. Wolf
(a) Wolve
(b) Wolfs
(c) Wolves
(d) None of the above

8. Baby
(a) Babys
(b) Babeis
(c) Babies
(d) None of the above

Directions (Q. Nos. 9-16) Read the words given below and identify their singular form from the given options.

9. Glasses
(a) Glasse (b) Glas
(c) Glass (d) None of these

10. Mangoes
(a) Mangoe (b) Mango
(c) Mangoue (d) Mangeo

11. Feet
(a) Foots (b) Foote
(c) Feets (d) Foot

12. Brushes
(a) Brushe (b) Brushs
(c) Brush (d) None of these

13. Classes
(a) Class
(b) Classe
(c) Clasess
(d) Clase

14. Watches

(a) Watche (b) Watchs
(c) Watch (d) Watchis

15. Armies

(a) Armi (b) Army
(c) Arme (d) Armie

16. Taxes

(a) Tax (b) Taxe
(c) Taxs (d) None of these

Directions (Q. Nos. 17-19) Fill in the blanks with correct options.

17. We saw a .... in the zoo.

(a) birds (b) animals
(c) bears (d) lion

18. We fed grains to ....

(a) elephant (b) tiger
(c) parrots (d) dog

19. I would like to have some ....

(a) leaves (b) cookies
(c) balls (d) coffees

Directions (Q.Nos. 20-22) Read the sentences given below and choose the plural form of the underlined words.

20. My mother lost her mobile.

(a) mobiles (b) mobilie
(c) mobile (d) mobil

21. Please add vegetable in the rice.

(a) vegetabels (b) vegetabled
(c) vegetables (d) None of these

22. Where is the sharp knife?

(a) knifes (b) knives
(c) knifese (d) knive

Directions (Q. Nos. 23-25) Read the sentences given below and choose the singular form of the underlined words.

23. Do you know where I kept my office files?

(a) fil (b) filen
(c) file (d) None of these

24. The judge invited wives of all the army men.

(a) wive (b) wife (c) wivs (d) wifes

25. Big clocks were put at the railway station.

(a) clockes (b) clock
(c) clockse (d) None of these

Directions (Q. Nos. 26 and 27) Find the number of singular and plural nouns in the given box.

Car, toys, cat, dog, bottles, pens, mouse, colours, paper, eraser, arms, toes, table, feet, tooth, finger, books, ring, bag, potatoes, men, child

26. There are .... singular nouns in the given box.

(a) 20 (b) 12 (c) 10 (d) 15

27. There are .... plural nouns in the given box.

(a) 18 (b) 16 (c) 10 (d) 14

Chapter 08

Masculine and Feminine (Gender)

Directions (Q. Nos. 1-10) Choose the correct feminine gender of the following words from the given options.

1. Emperor
(a) Lady (b) Empress
(c) Baby (d) Mother

2. Uncle
(a) Aunty (b) lady
(c) Woman (d) Female

3. Prince
(a) Queen (b) Madam
(c) Princess (d) Empress

4. Sir
(a) Mrs. (b) Madam
(c) Miss (d) Woman

5. Tiger
(a) Cub (b) Tiges
(c) Tigress (d) Lioness

6. Grandfather
(a) Mother (b) Grandmother
(c) Grandlady (d) Lady

7. Waiter
(a) Waites (b) Madam
(c) Waitress (d) Aunty

8. Nephew
(a) Niece (b) Brother
(c) Sister (d) Cousin

9. God
(a) Godlady (b) Goddess
(c) God woman (d) Female God

10. Hero
(a) Madame (b) Actress
(c) Heroine (d) Woman

Directions (Q. Nos. 11-15) Read the sentences given below and choose the correct feminine gender of the underlined word.

11. Rahul is Shilpa's <u>husband</u>.
(a) wive (b) wives (c) wife (d) lady

12. Uncle is my grandmother's <u>son-in-law</u>.
(a) woman (b) daughter
(c) daughter-in-law (d) wife

13. He was hit by an angry <u>bull</u>.
(a) calf (b) cow
(c) hen (d) deer

14. She is as clever as a <u>fox</u>.
(a) vixen (b) lioness
(c) foxess (d) foxy

15. Rita met a <u>witch</u> today.

(a) witchman (b) witcher
(c) wizard (d) witch

Directions (Q. Nos. 16-22) Choose the correct masculine gender of the following words from the given options.

16. Woman

(a) Boy (b) Man
(c) Uncle (d) Father

17. Bitch

(a) Deer (b) Hare
(c) Dog (d) Doe

18. Queen

(a) King (b) Prince
(c) Son (d) Emperor

19. Actress

(a) Hero (b) Actor
(c) Player (d) Lady

20. Bride

(a) Bridegroom (b) Bridal
(c) Bestman (d) Duke

21. Lady

(a) Lord (b) King
(c) Man (d) Emperor

22. Priestess

(a) God (b) Monk
(c) Priest (d) Nun

Directions (Q. Nos. 23-25) Read the sentences given below and choose the correct masculine gender of the underlined word from the given options.

23. In the mall I was looking for the <u>saleswoman</u>.

(a) sales person (b) salesman
(c) seller (d) saleslady

24. The <u>peahen</u> danced during the rain.

(a) peacheck (b) pearer
(c) peacock (d) peadon

25. The <u>washerwoman</u> comes to pick clothes daily.

(a) washerer (b) washerman
(c) washerlad (d) washerson

Chapter 09

Simple Tenses

Directions (Q.Nos. 1-10) Choose the present tense of the given words.

1. Walk
(a) Walks (b) Talks
(c) Hops (d) Jumps

2. Sleep
(a) Catches (b) Sleeps
(c) Wakes (d) Cares

3. Hold
(a) Slips (b) Throws
(c) Holds (d) Plays

4. Make
(a) Makes (b) Takes
(c) Shakes (d) Wastes

5. Play
(a) Hides (b) Guides
(c) Draws (d) Plays

6. Write
(a) Whites (b) Paints
(c) Writes (d) Walks

7. Run
(a) Buns (b) Runs
(c) Jumps (d) Wins

8. Drive
(a) Drives (b) Grows
(c) Falls (d) Calls

9. Build
(a) Tries (b) Builds
(c) Lays (d) Picks

10. Bend
(a) Knocks (b) Sits
(c) Stands (d) Bends

Directions (Q.Nos. 11-20) Choose the past tense of the given words.

11. Eat
(a) Ate (b) Bate
(c) Eated (d) Beated

12. Sleep
(a) Cleaned (b) Sleeped
(c) Slept (d) Walked

13. Talk
(a) Shaked (b) Talked
(c) Pinned (d) Canned

14. Give
(a) Gave (b) Gived
(c) Taked (d) Take

15. Play
(a) Baked (b) Shook
(c) Made (d) Played

16. Sit
(a) Bat (b) Sat
(c) Sitted (d) Mat

17. Write

(a) Wrote (b) Vote

(c) Cleared (d) Packed

18. Draw

(a) Painted (b) Drew

(c) Picked (d) Ran

19. Drink

(a) Drinked (b) Drank

(c) Bank (d) Hanged

20. Sing

(a) Sang (b) Song

(c) Dried (d) Cried

Directions (Q.Nos. 21-25) Fill in the blanks with present tense of the words.

21. Simmi .... to the school.

(a) talks (b) walks

(c) writes (d) lives

22. He .... up early in the morning.

(a) goes (b) ties

(c) wakes (d) sleeps

23. Shreya .... water.

(a) drinks (b) eats

(c) draws (d) plays

24. They .... for this company.

(a) do (b) finish

(c) work (d) complete

25. Two .... two is equals to four.

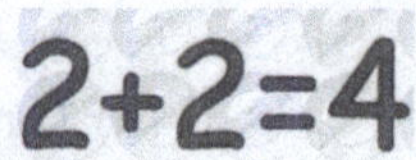

(a) works (b) writes

(c) divides (d) adds

Directions (Q.Nos. 26-28) Fill in the blanks with past tense of the words.

26. I .... my room.

(a) cleaned (b) lived

(c) slept (d) talked

27. Rohan .... a glass of milk.

(a) ate (b) threw

(c) drank (d) completed

28. The monkey .... the banana.

(a) pulled (b) caught

(c) got (d) ate

Chapter 10

Words and their Meanings

Directions (Q. Nos. 1-10) Choose the word similar in meaning to the given words.

1. Garbage
   (a) Trash (b) Flies
   (c) Packet (d) Bin

2. Dusty
   (a) Soil (b) Dirty
   (c) Boy (d) Cap

3. Incorrect
   (a) Right (b) Tight
   (c) Cross (d) Wrong

4. Flame
   (a) Woods (b) Match
   (c) Fire (d) Hot

5. Celebration
   (a) Bake (b) Enjoy
   (c) Party (d) Whistle

6. Gentle
   (a) Pillow (b) Square
   (c) Cushion (d) Soft

7. Present
   (a) Toy (b) Gift
   (c) Box (d) Ribbon

8. Correct
   (a) Right (b) Write
   (c) Left (d) Tick

9. Hard
   (a) Stone (b) Round
   (c) Solid (d) Rough

10. Gate
    (a) Door (b) Knob
    (c) Rectangle (d) Wall

Directions (Q. Nos. 11-14) Select the pair of similar words from the following.

11. (a) Kind and nice (b) Mean and sad
    (c) Kind and mean (d) Sad and nice

12. (a) Eat and pal (b) Friend and eat
    (c) Pal and friend (d) Play and pal

13. Close, Far, Fear, Near, Dear
    (a) Close and Fear (b) Far and Near
    (c) Close and Near (d) Fear and Near

14. Simple, Easy, Quite, Tough, Hard
    (a) Simple and Easy
    (b) Easy and Tough
    (c) Easy and Quite
    (d) Simple and Hard

15. Match the following in List I with the similar meaning words in List II.

List I		List II	
A.	Choose	1.	Fix
B.	Mend	2.	Happy
C.	Simple	3.	Select
D.	Joyful	4.	Easy

Codes

	A	B	C	D
(a)	1	4	3	2
(b)	3	1	4	2
(c)	3	1	2	4
(d)	1	3	4	2

Directions (Q. Nos. 16 and 17) Complete the missing letters to make words that mean the same.

16. GL_W SH_NE
(a) Glew and Shine
(b) Glow and Shine
(c) Glaw and Shane
(d) Glow and Shene

17. S_A_L T_N_
(a) Snail and Ting
(b) Small and Ting
(c) Small and Tiny
(d) Snail and Tiny

Directions (Q. Nos. 18-24) Choose the similar word for the underlined words.

18. We took a <u>taxi</u> to go to Agra.
(a) Cab (b) Cap
(c) Back (d) Car

19. I like to have <u>sweets</u>.
(a) Dish (b) Plate
(c) Dessert (d) Fruit

20. He went to Shimla for a <u>trip</u>.
(a) Fall (b) Hide
(c) Go (d) Vacation

21. She is <u>unhappy</u> because she lost her doll.
(a) Happy (b) Excited
(c) Sad (d) Enjoying

22. A <u>lady</u> is crossing the road.
(a) Woman (b) Aunt
(c) Man (d) Animal

23. This test is not very <u>difficult</u>.
(a) Easy (b) Long
(c) Hard (d) Short

24. She is my <u>friend</u>.
(a) Pal (b) Brother
(c) Enemy (d) Aunt

25. Match the words given in List I with words similar in meaning given in List II.

List I		List II	
A.	Toss	1.	Loved
B.	Move	2.	Throw
C.	Cry	3.	Walk
D.	Dear	4.	Weep

Codes

	A	B	C	D		A	B	C	D
(a)	1	2	3	4	(b)	2	3	4	1
(c)	2	4	3	1	(d)	2	1	3	4

Chapter 11

Words and their Opposites

Directions (Q.Nos. 1-10) Choose the word opposite in meaning to the given words.

1. Clean
(a) Neat (b) Dirty
(c) Tidy (d) Simple

2. Bent
(a) Straight (b) Rough
(c) One (d) Single

3. Soft
(a) Pillow (b) Gentle
(c) Stone (d) Hard

4. Sweet
(a) Sour (b) Bitter
(c) Ugly (d) Tastty

5. Beautiful
(a) Sad (b) Pretty
(c) Ugly (d) Happy

6. Down
(a) Side (b) Left
(c) Up (d) Right

7. Old
(a) Fresh (b) New
(c) Time (d) Half

8. Float
(a) Fly (b) Walk
(c) Sink (d) Fall

9. Stop
(a) Wait (b) Go (c) Rest (d) End

10. Heavy
(a) Small (b) Soft (c) Light (d) Push

Directions (Q. Nos. 11-20) Choose the correct opposite word for the given words.

11. Like
(a) Fake (b) New
(c) Old (d) Dislike

12. Hate
(a) Angry (b) Sad (c) Love (d) Shy

13. Many
(a) Lots of (b) Few
(c) Much (d) More

14. Easy
(a) Difficult (b) Simple
(c) Rough (d) Plane

15. In
(a) Inside (b) Up (c) Down (d) Out

16. Push

(a) Empty (b) Pull
(c) Stop (d) Heavy

17. Fast

(a) Write (b) Slow
(c) Jump (d) Run

18. Forget

(a) Upset (b) Reminder
(c) Remember (d) Remain

19. War

(a) Flowers (b) Peace
(c) Angry (d) Happiness

20. Active

(a) Lazy (b) Less
(c) Lean (d) Cute

21. Match the words given in List I with the words opposite in meaning given in List II.

List I	List II
A. Right	1. Dishonest
B. Honest	2. Left
C. Easy	3. Slow
D. Fast	4. Difficult

Codes

	A	B	C	D
(a)	1	3	2	4
(b)	2	1	3	4
(c)	2	1	4	3
(d)	2	3	1	4

22. Match the words given in List I with the words opposite in meaning given in List II.

List I	List II
A. Clear	1. Close
B. True	2. False
C. Move	3. Unclear
D. Open	4. Stop

Codes

	A	B	C	D		A	B	C	D
(a)	3	2	4	1	(b)	3	1	2	4
(c)	3	4	2	1	(d)	3	2	1	4

Directions (Q. Nos. 23-25) Fill in the blanks with opposite word of the underlined words.

23. When my glass of milk is ...., I fill it up again until it is full.

(a) blank (b) empty
(c) hole (d) space

24. We go in through the front door and we go out through the .... door.

(a) behind (b) ahead
(c) back (d) previous

25. The apples are .... in comparison to light weight cotton balls.

(a) hard (b) thick
(c) thin (d) heavy

Directions (Q. Nos. 26-30) Select the opposite word of the underlined words in the following sentences.

26. This is a cheap gift.

(a) Cost (b) Expensive
(c) Good (d) Bold

27. I met a foolish man.

(a) Brave (b) Wise
(c) Fool (d) Happy

28. Ravi is young.

(a) Older (b) Infant
(c) Old (d) Bold

29. This book is very boring.

(a) Interesting (b) Funny
(c) Sad (d) Happy

30. Why are you crying?

(a) Smile (b) Sleeping
(c) Talking (d) Laughing

Chapter 12

Jumbled Words

Directions (Q. Nos. 1-10) Identify the correct formation of word.

1. (a) Bbul
   (b) Bulb
   (c) Blub
   (d) Blbu

2. (a) Fish
   (b) Shif
   (c) Ifsh
   (d) Hifs

3. (a) Rainwob
   (b) Airnbow
   (c) Rainbow
   (d) Brainwo

4. (a) Henoyeeb
   (b) Hnyeoebe
   (c) Beeyonhe
   (d) Honeybee

5. (a) Cilpen
   (b) Pencil
   (c) Neplic
   (d) Plicen

6. 

   (a) Lowerfs (b) Flowres
   (c) Flowers (d) Ewlfors

7. (a) Ladybug
   (b) Buglady
   (c) Bluadyg
   (d) Dugbaly

8. (a) Lockc
   (b) Clock
   (c) Clokc
   (d) Kolcc

9. (a) Kace
   (b) Acck
   (c) Cake
   (d) ekac

10. (a) Rryche
    (b) Cherry
    (c) Herryc
    (d) Hercyr

Directions (Q. Nos. 11-20) Rearrange the following jumbled words to make meaningful words.

11. PYPUP
    (a) PPUPY
    (b) PUPY
    (c) Puppy
    (d) PUPYP

12. ESHUO
    (a) Shout (b) Louse
    (c) Douse (d) House

13. RNATI

(a) Again (b) Train

(c) Plain (d) Brain

14. TMCOE

(a) Cart (b) Comet

(c) Vomit (d) Muscat

15. CHNUM

(a) Punch (b) Bunch

(c) Munch (d) Crunch

16. RIEFDN

(a) Trend (b) Differ

(c) Friend (d) Fiernd

17. RAPGSE

(a) Plates (b) Gape

(c) Shape (d) Grapes

18. AHCPE

(a) Chair (b) Peach

(c) Cheap (d) Clean

19. MALSL

(a) SMAL (b) LASML

(c) Stall (d) Small

20. RYTEPT

(a) Priety (b) Pretty

(c) Pettry (d) Reptty

Directions (Q. Nos. 21-25) Fill in the blanks with correctly spelt words.

21. We travelled to Europe by ....

(a) aeropanle (b) aeroplane

(c) planeaero (d) laneproea

22. I am washing ....

(a) lothesc (b) clohest

(c) clothes (d) sothecl

23. The .... ploughs the field.

(a) armfer (b) farrem

(c) merfarm (d) farmer

24. I have a pink ....

(a) frock (b) rofck

(c) korfc (d) orfck

25. Sheetal has cleaned her ....

(a) moor (b) omor

(c) room (d) romo

Chapter 13

Words Pair and Odd One Out

1. Select the balloon which has a pair of rhyming words.

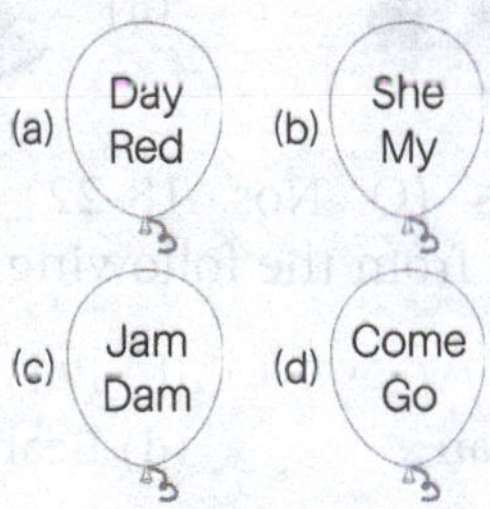

2. The rhyming word which completes the series.

Roam, Loam, ...

(a) Room (b) Loan
(c) Gone (d) Foam

3. Complete the missing letters of the rhyming words given in the kite.

(a) Gate (b) Gatd
(c) Gait (d) Gata

4. Which of the following sets of words do not rhyme?

(a) Fool, Cool, Pool (b) Mane, Lane, Jane
(c) Just, Must, Last (d) Show, Blow, Mow

5. Fill in the blanks to make the rhyming word pair.

DREAM _ _ EAM

(a) CT (b) CR
(c) LS (d) BE

6. Find out the two rhyming words from the box.

Cat, plum, clap, drum, bun, dote

(a) Cat and Bun (b) Drum and Bun
(c) Plum and Drum (d) Dote and Cat

7. Look at the pictures below. The name of two of the pictures rhyme with each other. What are they?

(1) (2) (3) (4)

(a) 1 and 2 (b) 2 and 3
(c) 2 and 4 (d) 3 and 4

8. Select the word that fits the series.
bun, fun, pun, ...
(a) jan (b) gun (c) men (d) dam

Directions (Q. Nos. 9-13) Complete the word pairs.

9. Knife and ....
(a) Spoon
(b) Bowl
(c) Fork
(d) Plate

10. .... and write
(a) See
(b) Book
(c) Paper
(d) Read

11. Up and ....
(a) Stairs
(b) Down
(c) Monkey
(d) Happy

12. .... and pepper
(a) Black
(b) Salt
(c) Bottle
(d) Spray

13. Bride and ....
(a) Groom
(b) Man
(c) Boy
(d) Uncle

Directions (Q. Nos. 14-17) Choose the odd one out from given pictures/words.

14. (a)  (b) 
(c)  (d) 

15. (a)  (b) 
(c)  (d) 

16. (a) Red (b) Green
(c) Blue (d) 

17. (a)  (b) 
(c)  (d) 

Directions (Q. Nos. 18-22) Choose the odd one out from the following.

18. (a) Cat (b) Rat
(c) Aman (d) Bear

19. (a) Come
(b) Hay
(c) Play
(d) Day

20. (a) Kota
(b) Delhi
(c) Home
(d) Jaipur

21. (a) Drive
(b) Hive
(c) Beef
(d) Jive

22. (a) Cherry
(b) Carrot
(c) Banana
(d) Grapes

Chapter 14

Spelling Test

Directions (Q. Nos. 1-10) Choose the correct spelling.

1. 

(a) Batub (b) Bathtub
(c) Bathtab (d) Bathetub

2. 

(a) Kloc (b) Cloc
(c) Clock (d) Klock

3. 

(a) Crayons
(b) Creyons
(c) Cryons
(d) Craiyons

4. 

(a) Bubbel (b) Bebbel
(c) Bubble (d) Bubal

5. 

(a) Yatch (b) Yacht
(c) Yaut (d) Yautch

6. 

(a) Iglu (b) Igaloo
(c) Egloo (d) Igloo

7. 

(a) Wheel (b) Weel
(c) Weal (d) Wheal

8. 

(a) Buterfly (b) Batarfly
(c) Butterfly (d) Buttarfli

9. 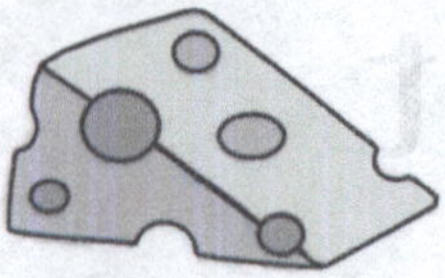

(a) Chease (b) Cheese
(c) Chise (d) Chaese

10. 

(a) Kattle (b) Katle
(c) Kettle (d) Cettle

Directions (Q. Nos. 11-15) Choose the correct spellings from the given words.

11. (a) Blown (b) Bloan
(c) Blon (d) Bloun

12. (a) Trapp (b) Trap
(c) Trep (d) Traip

13. (a) Airoplain (b) Aeroplain
(c) Aeroplane (d) Airoplane

14. (a) Bottal (b) Bottle
(c) Botal (d) Bottel

15. (a) Saucepan (b) Saucepen
(c) Socepan (d) Sauspan

Directions (Q. Nos. 16-20) Choose the wrongly spelt word.

16. (a) Clown (b) Napkin
(c) Tractar (d) Mice

17. (a) Simpal (b) Drive
(c) Fire (d) Street

18. (a) Grain (b) Umbrella
(c) Sprey (d) Church

19. (a) Elephant (b) Tiger
(c) Silver (d) Crocodail

20. (a) Brother (b) Famili
(c) Mirror (d) Remote

Directions (Q. Nos. 21-25) Fill in the blanks with correctly spelt words.

21. My .... is red in colour.
(a) hause (b) house
(c) houce (d) hauce

22. Siya loves to eat ....
(a) ice crim
(b) icy creem
(c) ice creem
(d) ice cream

23. A doctor works in a ....
(a) hospital (b) hospitel
(c) hospeetal (d) hospittal

24. The .... is open.
(a) windo (b) window
(c) windew (d) windoh

25. Our .... is delayed by 2 hours.
(a) traen (b) trean
(c) trane (d) train

Chapter 15

Animal and their Babies, Sounds, Home & Group

Directions (Q. Nos. 1-5) Choose the young ones of the following animals from the options given below.

1. Bird
   (a) Birdie (b) Birdling
   (c) Small bird (d) Chick

2. Tiger
   (a) Tigress (b) Ape
   (c) Cub (d) Bunny

3. Cat
   (a) Baby cat (b) Kitten
   (c) Kitty (d) Cub

4. Duck
   (a) Duckling (b) Chick
   (c) Birdling (d) Doll

5. Frog
   (a) Froggie (b) Tadpole
   (c) Baby frog (d) Doll

Directions (Q. Nos. 6-10) Choose the correct sound made by the animals from the options given below.

6. Dogs
   (a) Cry (b) Chirp
   (c) Bark (d) Roar

7. Elephants
   (a) Quack (b) Hiss
   (c) Moo (d) Trumpet

8. Lions
   (a) Hiss (b) Roar
   (c) Bleat (d) Snort

9. Horse
   (a) Chirp (b) Bark
   (c) Neigh (d) Chatter

10. Duck
    (a) Coo (b) Quack
    (c) Scream (d) Buzz

Directions (Q. Nos. 11-13) Choose the name of houses of the given animals or birds.

11. Dogs
    (a) Aquarium (b) Coops
    (c) Kennel (d) Nest

12. Bird
    (a) Hole (b) Cobwebs
    (c) Nest (d) Water

13. Mouse
    (a) Ant hill (b) Hole
    (c) Den (d) Nest

14. Match the animals in List A with the name of their younger ones in List B. Choose the answer from the given options.

List A	List B
A. Deer	1. Calf
B. Fox	2. Duckling
C. Cow	3. Fawn
D. Duck	4. Cub

Codes

	A	B	C	D
(a)	4	2	3	1
(b)	3	4	1	2
(c)	4	1	2	3
(d)	2	3	1	4

Directions (Q. Nos. 15-19) Choose the correct animal groups from the options given below.

15. Lions

(a) Herd (b) Troops
(c) Pride (d) Flock

16. Wolves

(a) Drove (b) Pack
(c) Streak (d) Barrel

17. Buffaloes

(a) Colony (b) Herd
(c) Tribe (d) Team

18. Butterfly

(a) Pride (b) Swarm
(c) Pod (d) Herd

19. Fish

(a) Horde
(b) School
(c) Litter
(d) Flock

Directions (Q.Nos. 20-24) Choose the correct option to fill in the blanks.

20. A baby tiger is called a ....

(a) calf (b) foal (c) kid (d) cub

21. Horse lives in a ....

(a) kennel (b) stable
(c) shed (d) cave

22. Ducks like to swim in a ....

(a) pond (b) mud
(c) jungle (d) aquarium

23. A .... does baa-baa and its baby is called lamb.

(a) goat (b) deer (c) sheep (d) fox

24. A group of .... is called a herd.

(a) wolves (b) fish
(c) rabbits (d) elephants

Chapter 16

Reading Comprehension

Directions (Q. Nos. 1-5) Read the following passage and answer the questions that follow.

A little girl was going to school. She met an injured dog on the way. She took the dog to a nearby hospital. The doctor treated the dog and gave medicines so that the dog could get well. The girl took the dog to her home and gave him food to eat. After few days the dog got well. The little girl and the dog became good friends.

1. Whom did the little girl meet on her way to school?
(a) Puppy (b) Friend
(c) Dog (d) Magician

2. Where did she take the dog?
(a) House (b) Market
(c) Garden (d) Hospital

3. The dog was ....
(a) barking (b) angry
(c) happy (d) injured

4. The opposite of 'well' is
(a) unwell (b) angry
(c) sad (d) swell

5. A word that means similar to 'friend' is
(a) enemy (b) pal
(c) follower (d) grand

Directions (Q. Nos. 6-10) Read the following passage and answer the questions that follow.

A hen had two chicks. Their names were Lalu and Peelu. Lalu loved red things. Peelu loved yellow things. One day Lalu ate a red chilli. It was very hot. Lalu started crying. Peelu gave him a yellow laddu to eat. Lalu stopped crying after eating it. Mother Hen and Lalu kissed Peelu.

6. What things did Peelu love?
(a) Red things
(b) Green things
(c) White things
(d) Yellow things

7. The yellow laddu was
(a) bitter (b) hot
(c) sweet (d) tasteless

8. How was the chilli?
(a) Very hot (b) Hot
(c) Very cold (d) Cold

9. What did Peelu give Lalu?

(a) Banana (b) Laddu

(c) Water (d) Toffee

10. Why did Mother hen and Lalu kiss Peelu?

(a) As he had done a bad thing

(b) As he wanted to be kissed

(c) As he had helped Lalu

(d) None of the above

Directions (Q. Nos. 11-15) Read the following passage and answer the questions that follow.

A woodpecker is the king of birds. Woodpeckers are found all over the world except in the North and South poles, Australia and New Zealand. There are over 200 different kinds of woodpeckers. The two largest woodpeckers, the Imperial Woodpecker and the Ivory-billed Woodpecker are most likely extinct. Animals that are extinct are no longer found on Earth.

Woodpeckers have sharp bills for drilling into wood and short, stiff tails which help prop them up against tree trunks and branches. Woodpeckers also have very long tongues, which help them get at insects deep within trees.

11. Where do we find woodpeckers?

(a) Australia

(b) All over the world except some places

(c) India

(d) South Pole

12. Why do woodpeckers have long tongues?

(a) To eat seeds (b) To get an insect

(c) To eat fruit (d) To cut the wood

13. What does the word 'extinct' mean?

(a) Dead

(b) Rare bird

(c) No longer found on Earth

(d) Found everywhere

14. The word 'sharp' may also mean

(a) dull (b) clever

(c) pointed (d) piercing

15. The opposite of 'stiff' is

(a) soft (b) lose (c) hard (d) plastic

Directions (Q. Nos. 16-20) Read the following passage and answer the questions that follow.

A mother sparrow lived, with the two chicks, in a wheat field. The chicks soon learnt to hop and fly. They would hop and drop and then go flap, flap, flap, flap! One day the chicks said, "Mom, let us fly away. The farmer will soon cut the wheat."

The mother said, "No, no! The farmer is not ready." And after some days the farmer brought his friends to the field and he said, "Will you help me cut the wheat?" and the friends said: Oh! Yes! The chicks again asked their mother, "Shall we fly away?" And the mother said: "Yes, Yes, we must fly away before farmer cuts the wheat".

16. Where did the mother sparrow live?

(a) In a tree (b) In a house

(c) In a wheat field (d) On the road

17. What did the chicks suggest to mother one day?

(a) Let us run (b) Let us fly

(c) Let us swim (d) Let us eat

18. Whom did the farmer bring one day to the field?

(a) His dog (b) His father

(c) His friends (d) His children

19. What is the opposite of 'soon'?

(a) Far (b) Never

(c) Slow (d) Quick

20. The word 'ready' can also mean
(a) slow (b) prepared
(c) smart (d) fast

Directions (Q. Nos. 21-25) Read the passage and answer the questions that follow.

Gopu had a pet cat. The cat's name was Lily. Gopu played with Lily when he came from school. He gave it many nice things to eat. One day Lily went out of the house. Gopu cried when he did not find her after coming from school. He searched her near his house and found her stuck on the top of a tree. Lily did not know how to come down the tree. Gopu climbed the tree and brought her down. They both were very happy.

21. What pet did Gopu have?
(a) Dog (b) Kitten
(c) Rabbit (d) Cat

22. What did Gopu give Lily to eat?
(a) Chicken (b) Sugar
(c) Nice things (d) Milk

23. Where did Gopu find Lily?
(a) On a roof top (b) On a donkey
(c) On a tree top (d) On a horse

24. The opposite of the word 'down' is
(a) in (b) up
(c) out (d) first

25. A word that means similar to 'happy' is
(a) joyful (b) sad (c) bad (d) mean

Directions (Q. Nos. 26-30) Read the following poem and answer the questions that follow.

Apples, apples,
Growing on a tree.
Apples, apples
Pick one just for me!
Apples, apples,
Tasty as can be,
Apples, apples,
Share one now with me!

26. What are growing on the tree?
(a) Bananas (b) Plums
(c) Mangoes (d) Apples

27. The child wants .... apple.
(a) two (b) three (c) one (d) four

28. How are the apples?
(a) Tasteless (b) Tasty
(c) Rotten (d) Stolen

29. A word that means the same as 'tasty' is
(a) sour (b) delicious
(c) foul-smelling (d) dear

30. A word that rhymes with 'just' is
(a) must (b) best
(c) more (d) near

Chapter 17

Communication Skills

Directions (Q.Nos. 1-10) Fill in the blanks appropriate words.

1. When someone says 'Hello' to you, you should say ....
(a) Goodbye (b) Hello
(c) Good night (d) Go away

2. What do you say when you get a gift?
(a) Thank you (b) Sorry
(c) Hello (d) Please

3. How do you greet everyone after waking up?
(a) Good night (b) Good bye
(c) Hello (d) Good morning

4. What do you say before going to bed?
(a) Good night (b) Good evening
(c) Good morning (d) Good afternoon

5. If you make a mistake, you would say ....
(a) Thank you (b) Sorry
(c) Nice (d) Please

6. When your friend leaves your house you would say ....
(a) Bye (b) Welcome
(c) Come in (d) Wow

7. If someone says 'Thank you', you would say ....
(a) No (b) Yes
(c) Ok (d) Welcome

8. If someone says 'Sorry' to you, you would say ....
(a) I'm fine (b) Go away
(c) It's ok (d) I'm good

9. When you request, you would say ....
(a) Thank you (b) Please
(c) Yes (d) I want it

10. If you want to get people out of your way, you would say ....
(a) Get away (b) Get out of my way
(c) Excuse me (d) Please get away

Directions (Q.Nos. 11-15) This is the picture of a doctor. Answer the following questions based on the picture.

11. When we .... ill we go to a doctor.

(a) is (b) are
(c) were (d) was

12. The doctor checks carefully .... any illness.

(a) on (b) in (c) for (d) of

13. He works in a ....

(a) house (b) school
(c) hospital (d) office

14. He gives medicines to the ....

(a) mother (b) children
(c) patients (d) principal

15. The doctor is very ....

(a) rude (b) angry
(c) polite (d) friendly

Directions (Q. Nos. 16-20) Complete the conversations

16.

(a) Yes (b) No
(c) Sure (d) Thank you

17.

(a) Yes (b) Yes, sure
(c) Sure (d) No

18.

(a) Ok (b) Nice
(c) Thank you (d) Sorry

19.

(a) Who are you?
(b) I am fine.
(c) Don't talk to me.
(d) Bye

20.

(a) I am shocked.
(b) I don't know.
(c) I am going.
(d) I can't tell you.

PRACTICE SET 01

1. Find the noun(s) in the following sentence.
Kamal went to visit the zoo in a car.
(a) Kamal (b) zoo
(c) car (d) All of these

2. Match the following with their plurals.

List I	List II
A. Loaf	1. Postmen
B. Puppy	2. Loaves
C. Deer	3. Puppies
D. Postman	4. Deer

Codes

	A	B	C	D		A	B	C	D
(a)	2	3	4	1	(b)	2	3	1	4
(c)	1	2	3	4	(d)	4	3	2	1

3. Find the number of pronouns in the following lines.
Rajan went to the school. There he met his friends. They asked him to give a party as he had came first in school.
(a) 4 (b) 5 (c) 3 (d) 6

4. Which of the following is a verb?
(a) Fine (b) Line (c) Dine (d) Nine

5. Fill in the blank using articles.
...... elephant went to meet ...... deer.
(a) A, a (b) An, a
(c) A, an (d) The, the

6. Find the preposition(s) in the following sentence.
A Deer fell into the well while looking for food.
(a) A (b) while (c) for (d) A, for

7. Fill in the blank with a suitable adjective.
Raman purchased a .... suit for his birthday.
(a) old (b) new
(c) torn (d) worn out

8. Re-arrange the following jumbled letters to make a meaningful word.
ASRCE
(a) SARCE (b) SCEAR
(c) SCARE (d) SRACE

9. Find the odd one out.
(a) Light (b) Torch (c) Bulb (d) Candle

10. Complete the series.
Plan, Clan, ...
(a) Ban (b) Men
(c) Drain (d) Blunder

11. Match the following animals with their young ones.

List I	List II
A. Dog	1. Calf
B. Horse	2. Puppy
C. Tiger	3. Foal
D. Cow	4. Cub

Codes

	A	B	C	D		A	B	C	D
(a)	2	3	1	4	(b)	4	3	2	1
(c)	2	3	4	1	(d)	1	2	3	4

12. What is a group of buffaloes called?

(a) Flock (b) Herd

(c) Pack (d) Army

13. What sound does an owl make?

(a) Chirp (b) Chatter

(c) Hoot (d) Meow

Directions (Q. Nos. 14-17) This is the picture of a cloud. Answer the questions that follow based on this picture.

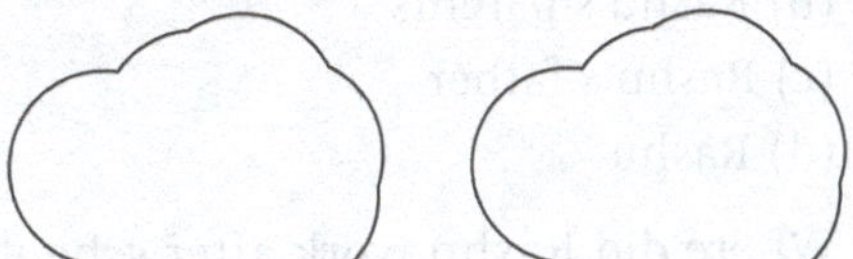

14. There are many clouds...... the sky.

(a) on (b) in

(c) into (d) above

15. Usually, the clouds are ...... in colour.

(a) white (b) yellow

(c) black (d) blue

16. The clouds .... of different shapes and sizes.

(a) is (b) am

(c) are (d) was

17. We get rains .... clouds.

(a) form (b) in

(c) on (d) from

18. Which of the following is the plural of dress?

(a) Dresses

(b) Dressis

(c) Dress

(d) Both (a) and (b)

19. Choose the correct option.

(a) Raman is a common noun.

(b) City is a proper noun.

(c) Rashi and Renu are proper nouns.

(d) School and hospital are collective nouns.

20. Fill in the blank with a suitable verb.

A tailor .... clothes and a barber cuts hair.

(a) stitch (b) stitches

(c) stitched (d) Stitchs

21. Choose the word similar in meaning to taxi?

(a) Cab (b) Car

(c) Bus (d) Train

22. Choose the feminine of horse.

(a) Mayor (b) Foal

(c) Stallion (d) Mare

23. Choose the opposite word of harmful.

(a) Danger (b) Safe

(c) Dangerous (d) Clean

24. Choose the correct spelling.

(a) Capsicam (b) Cepsicam

(c) Capsicum (d) Cepsicum

25. Choose the word with incorrect spelling.

(a) Himalayas (b) Singar

(c) Doctor (d) Mountains

26. Choose the masculine of washerwoman.

(a) Washerman

(b) Hewasher

(c) Washman

(d) Hewasherman

27. Complete the word pair.
Bread and ....
(a) knife (b) butter
(c) jam (d) tea

28. When you have to make a request you should say ....
(a) Thank you (b) Sorry
(c) Please (d) Excuse me

29. Complete the following dialogue.
Varun : Hello, Kapil.
Kapil : ....
(a) Hey there (b) Bye
(c) Hi (d) Hello, Varun

30. Fill in the blank with the correctly spelt word.
Shanu plays .... quite well.
(a) gitar (b) giutar
(c) guitar (d) gittar

Directions (Q. Nos. 31-35) Read the following passage and answer the questions that follow.

Rashu was in Class I. His parents were very poor. He had to go to school in the day and had to work in a factory after school. Whatever he earned was given in his school fees. He always stood first in class and wanted to become a doctor when he grew up.

31. What did Rashu do in the day?
(a) Went to school
(b) Went to college
(c) Went to a shop
(d) Went to a hospital

32. He had to work in a factory after school. 'He' in the above sentence stands for
(a) Rashu's teacher
(b) Rashu's parents
(c) Rashu's father
(d) Rashu

33. Where did Rashu work after school?
(a) In a shop
(b) In a factory
(c) In a stadium
(d) In a plant nursery

34. What is the opposite of 'first'?
(a) Second
(b) Lasted
(c) Last
(d) Second last

35. What kind of noun is 'Rashu'?
(a) Common noun
(b) Proper noun
(c) Collective noun
(d) Countable noun

PRACTICE SET 02

1. How many nouns are there in the passage below?
Shweta and Sara are friends. They go to school by bus. Their school is in the city and their house is far from their school.
(a) 7 (b) 5 (c) 6 (d) 4

2. Find the plural of the underlined words in the sentence.
The <u>mayor</u> held a party at the <u>city</u> square.
(a) mayoress, city (b) mayors, cities
(c) mayors, citys (d) mayoress, citys

3. Fill in the blank using correct pronoun.
Dimple played with .... best friend.
(a) his (b) he
(c) her (d) him

4. Fill in the blank using appropriate verb.
Naina .... nothing yesterday as she had a fast.
(a) eat (b) eaten
(c) eated (d) ate

5. Fill in the blank using a suitable article.
.... Ganges is our holy river.
(a) A (b) The
(c) An (d) A or An

6. Find the preposition in the following sentence.
The train went through the tunnel.
(a) train (b) tunnel
(c) through (d) went

7. Underline the adjective(s) in the following sentence.
Kanishka is a smart and studious boy.
(a) smart (b) boy
(c) studious (d) smart, studious

8. Re-arrange the following letters to make a meaningful word.
LACNCE
(a) CALCEN (b) CELCAN
(c) CANCEL (d) CCLEAN

9. Complete the series.
dear, near, ...
(a) fear (b) dire (c) bright (d) fero

10. Fill the missing letters to find word that mean the following.
DUMB : F_O_IS_
(a) O, M, H (b) O, L, H
(c) U, L, H (d) L, T, H

11. Which of the following are a pair of opposites?
Kind, crude, kindly, unkind, good
(a) Kind and crude
(b) Kind and good
(c) Unkind and crude
(d) Kind and unkind

12. Choose the odd one out from the following.
Good, happy, tear, healthy, well
(a) Good
(b) Healthy
(c) Tear
(d) well

13. Where does a bee live?
(a) Den (b) Beehive
(c) Coop (d) Stable

14. Birds make the .... sound.
(a) hooting (b) roaring
(c) barking (d) chirping

15. A young one of a bird is called a ....
(a) chick (b) birdling
(c) baby bird (d) ape

16. Honey is to sweet as Tamarind is to ....
(a) very sweet (b) salty
(c) sour (d) very salty

Directions (Q. Nos. 17 and 18) This is the picture of the Sun. Answer the questions based on the picture given below.

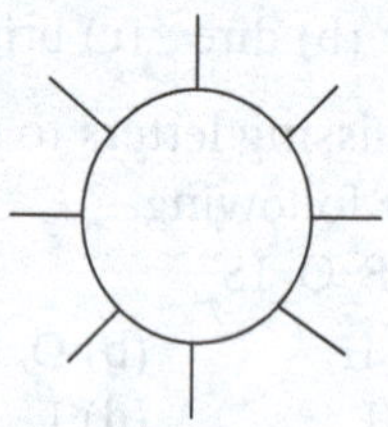

17. The picture is of .... Sun.
(a) a (b) an (c) the (d) as

18. The Sun .... in the morning.
(a) rise (b) risen (c) rose (d) rises

19. The plural of 'tomato' is
(a) tomatoes (b) tomatos
(c) tomats (d) tomates

20. Find the opposite gender of the underlined words.
The <u>hen</u> went to meet the <u>waiter</u>.
(a) cock, waitress
(b) hens, waiters
(c) he-hen, she-waiter
(d) henny, waiters

21. Choose the correct spelling.
(a) Valley (b) Valli
(c) Valey (d) Vailley

22. Choose the word similar in meaning to angry.
(a) Irritated (b) Furious
(c) Sad (d) Upset

23. Choose the word with incorrect spelling.
(a) Yacht (b) Watch
(c) Silver (d) Traingle

24. Choose the word similar in meaning to crying.
(a) Laughing (b) Smiling
(c) Weeping (d) Writing

25. Fill in the blank with correctly spelt word.
We went to Jaipur for ....
(a) Vecation (b) Vocation
(c) Veccation (d) Vacation

26. Unscramble the letters to form a meaningful word.
LASICSC
(a) SCISSOR (b) CLASS
(c) CLASSIC (d) LASICS

27. Choose the correct answer.
If you make a mistake you would say ....
(a) Thank you (b) Please
(c) Sorry (d) It's okay

28. Find the word opposite to bright.
(a) Glowing (b) Dull
(c) Simple (d) Old

29. Complete the following conversation.
A : ...., can you tell me the way to corridor?
B : Yes, sure.
(a) Sorry (b) Excuse me
(c) Please (d) Welcome

30. Choose the singular of the word 'feet'.
(a) Feets (b) Foots
(c) Foot (d) Fut

Directions (Q. Nos. 31-35) Read the following passage and answer the questions that follow.

A barber and a monkey became friends. The barber used to give the monkey bananas to eat. The monkey liked to eat bananas. The monkey used to climb on trees and pluck mangoes and apples and give it to the barber. The barber ate the fruits and thanked the monkey. One day the monkey fell ill. The barber took him to a doctor who treats animals. The monkey thought that the doctor would harm him and ran away. He never came back.

31. What did the barber gave the monkey?
(a) Mangoes (b) Apples
(c) Bananas (d) Plums

32. Why did the barber took the monkey to the doctor?
(a) Because the barber fell ill
(b) Because the monkey fell ill
(c) Because they wanted to play
(d) Because the doctor was their friend

33. The opposite of 'friends' is
(a) brother (b) cousin
(c) disciple (d) enemies

34. What did the monkey give the barber?
(a) Apples and mangoes
(b) Apples and bananas
(c) Mangoes and bananas
(d) Bananas

35. The plural of 'barber' is
(a) barberies
(b) barbers
(c) barberys
(d) barber

ANSWERS

Chapter 1 Nouns

1. (a)	**2.** (c)	**3.** (c)	**4.** (b)	**5.** (a)	**6.** (c)	**7.** (b)	**8.** (a)	**9.** (b)	**10.** (a)
11. (d)	**12.** (a)	**13.** (a)	**14.** (d)	**15.** (c)	**16.** (a)	**17.** (b)	**18.** (d)	**19.** (c)	**20.** (c)
21. (c)	**22.** (b)	**23.** (d)	**24.** (c)	**25.** (c)	**26.** (a)				

Chapter 2 Pronouns

1. (c)	**2.** (d)	**3.** (b)	**4.** (c)	**5.** (a)	**6.** (b)	**7.** (a)	**8.** (b)	**9.** (c)	**10.** (d)
11. (a)	**12.** (a)	**13.** (d)	**14.** (c)	**15.** (a)	**16.** (b)	**17.** (b)	**18.** (c)	**19.** (b)	**20.** (a)
21. (c)	**22.** (b)	**23.** (b)	**24.** (a)	**25.** (d)	**26.** (a)	**27.** (b)			

Chapter 3 Verbs

1. (b)	**2.** (a)	**3.** (b)	**4.** (c)	**5.** (d)	**6.** (b)	**7.** (a)	**8.** (c)	**9.** (d)	**10.** (b)
11. (c)	**12.** (b)	**13.** (a)	**14.** (b)	**15.** (d)	**16.** (b)	**17.** (c)	**18.** (b)	**19.** (c)	**20.** (a)
21. (c)									

Chapter 4 Adjectives

1. (b)	**2.** (b)	**3.** (a)	**4.** (c)	**5.** (d)	**6.** (d)	**7.** (a)	**8.** (b)	**9.** (c)	**10.** (d)
11. (d)	**12.** (b)	**13.** (c)	**14.** (a)	**15.** (c)	**16.** (b)	**17.** (c)	**18.** (a)	**19.** (d)	**20.** (c)
21. (a)									

Chapter 5 Articles

1. (b)	**2.** (a)	**3.** (c)	**4.** (a)	**5.** (b)	**6.** (b)	**7.** (c)	**8.** (a)	**9.** (b)	**10.** (a)
11. (b)	**12.** (a)	**13.** (a)	**14.** (d)	**15.** (a)	**16.** (b)	**17.** (c)	**18.** (b)	**19.** (b)	

Chapter 6 Prepositions

1. (b)	**2.** (c)	**3.** (a)	**4.** (c)	**5.** (b)	**6.** (c)	**7.** (d)	**8.** (a)	**9.** (b)	**10.** (c)
11. (b)	**12.** (c)	**13.** (b)	**14.** (d)	**15.** (b)	**16.** (a)	**17.** (c)	**18.** (b)		

Chapter 7 Singular and Plural

1. (b)	**2.** (a)	**3.** (c)	**4.** (a)	**5.** (c)	**6.** (b)	**7.** (c)	**8.** (c)	**9.** (c)	**10.** (b)
11. (d)	**12.** (c)	**13.** (a)	**14.** (c)	**15.** (b)	**16.** (a)	**17.** (d)	**18.** (c)	**19.** (b)	**20.** (a)
21. (c)	**22.** (b)	**23.** (c)	**24.** (b)	**25.** (b)	**26.** (b)	**27.** (c)			

Chapter 8 Feminine and Mesculine Gender

1. (b)	**2.** (a)	**3.** (c)	**4.** (b)	**5.** (c)	**6.** (b)	**7.** (c)	**8.** (a)	**9.** (b)	**10.** (c)
11. (c)	**12.** (c)	**13.** (b)	**14.** (a)	**15.** (c)	**16.** (b)	**17.** (c)	**18.** (a)	**19.** (b)	**20.** (a)
21. (a)	**22.** (c)	**23.** (b)	**24.** (c)	**25.** (b)					

Chapter 9 Simple Tenses

1. (a)	**2.** (b)	**3.** (c)	**4.** (a)	**5.** (d)	**6.** (c)	**7.** (b)	**8.** (a)	**9.** (b)	**10.** (d)
11. (a)	**12.** (c)	**13.** (b)	**14.** (a)	**15.** (d)	**16.** (b)	**17.** (a)	**18.** (b)	**19.** (b)	**20.** (a)
21. (b)	**22.** (c)	**23.** (a)	**24.** (c)	**25.** (d)	**26.** (a)	**27.** (c)	**28.** (d)		

Chapter 10 Words and their Meanings

1. (a)	**2.** (b)	**3.** (d)	**4.** (c)	**5.** (c)	**6.** (d)	**7.** (b)	**8.** (a)	**9.** (c)	**10.** (a)
11. (a)	**12.** (c)	**13.** (c)	**14.** (a)	**15.** (b)	**16.** (b)	**17.** (c)	**18.** (a)	**19.** (c)	**20.** (d)
21. (c)	**22.** (a)	**23.** (c)	**24.** (a)	**25.** (b)					

Chapter 11 Words and their Opposites

1. (b)	**2.** (a)	**3.** (d)	**4.** (b)	**5.** (c)	**6.** (c)	**7.** (b)	**8.** (c)	**9.** (b)	**10.** (c)
11. (d)	**12.** (c)	**13.** (b)	**14.** (a)	**15.** (d)	**16.** (b)	**17.** (b)	**18.** (c)	**19.** (b)	**20.** (a)
21. (c)	**22.** (a)	**23.** (b)	**24.** (c)	**25.** (d)	**26.** (b)	**27.** (b)	**28.** (c)	**29.** (a)	**30.** (d)

Chapter 12 Jumbled Words

1. (b)	**2.** (a)	**3.** (a)	**4.** (d)	**5.** (b)	**6.** (c)	**7.** (a)	**8.** (b)	**9.** (c)	**10.** (b)
11. (c)	**12.** (d)	**13.** (b)	**14.** (b)	**15.** (c)	**16.** (c)	**17.** (d)	**18.** (c)	**19.** (d)	**20.** (b)
21. (b)	**22.** (c)	**23.** (d)	**24.** (a)	**25.** (c)					

Chapter 13 Words Pair and Odd One Out

1. (c)	**2.** (d)	**3.** (a)	**4.** (c)	**5.** (b)	**6.** (c)	**7.** (c)	**8.** (b)	**9.** (c)	**10.** (d)
11. (b)	**12.** (b)	**13.** (a)	**14.** (d)	**15.** (d)	**16.** (d)	**17.** (d)	**18.** (c)	**19.** (a)	**20.** (c)
21. (c)	**22.** (b)								

Chapter 14 Spelling Test

1. (b)	**2.** (c)	**3.** (a)	**4.** (c)	**5.** (b)	**6.** (d)	**7.** (a)	**8.** (c)	**9.** (b)	**10.** (c)
11. (a)	**12.** (b)	**13.** (c)	**14.** (b)	**15.** (a)	**16.** (c)	**17.** (a)	**18.** (c)	**19.** (d)	**20.** (b)
21. (b)	**22.** (d)	**23.** (a)	**24.** (b)	**25.** (d)					

Chapter 15 Animal World and Their Babies, Sounds and Home

1. (d) **2.** (c) **3.** (b) **4.** (a) **5.** (b) **6.** (c) **7.** (d) **8.** (b) **9.** (c) **10.** (b)

11. (c) **12.** (c) **13.** (b) **14.** (b) **15.** (c) **16.** (b) **17.** (b) **18.** (b) **19.** (b) **20.** (d)

21. (b) **22.** (a) **23.** (c) **24.** (d)

Chapter 16 Reading Comprehension

1. (c) **2.** (d) **3.** (d) **4.** (a) **5.** (b) **6.** (d) **7.** (c) **8.** (a) **9.** (b) **10.** (c)

11. (b) **12.** (b) **13.** (c) **14.** (c) **15.** (a) **16.** (c) **17.** (b) **18.** (c) **19.** (b) **20.** (b)

21. (d) **22.** (c) **23.** (c) **24.** (b) **25.** (a) **26.** (d) **27.** (c) **28.** (b) **29.** (b) **30.** (a)

Chapter 17 Communication Skills

1. (b) **2.** (a) **3.** (d) **4.** (a) **5.** (b) **6.** (a) **7.** (d) **8.** (c) **9.** (b) **10.** (c)

11. (b) **12.** (c) **13.** (c) **14.** (c) **15.** (d) **16.** (b) **17.** (b) **18.** (c) **19.** (b) **20.** (b)

Practice Set 1

1. (d) **2.** (a) **3.** (b) **4.** (c) **5.** (b) **6.** (c) **7.** (b) **8.** (c) **9.** (d) **10.** (a)

11. (c) **12.** (b) **13.** (c) **14.** (b) **15.** (a) **16.** (c) **17.** (d) **18.** (a) **19.** (c) **20.** (b)

21. (a) **22.** (d) **23.** (b) **24.** (c) **25.** (b) **26.** (a) **27.** (b) **28.** (c) **29.** (d) **30.** (c)

31. (a) **32.** (d) **33.** (b) **34.** (c) **35.** (b)

Practice Set 2

1. (a) **2.** (b) **3.** (c) **4.** (d) **5.** (b) **6.** (c) **7.** (d) **8.** (c) **9.** (a) **10.** (b)

11. (d) **12.** (c) **13.** (b) **14.** (d) **15.** (a) **16.** (c) **17.** (c) **18.** (d) **19.** (a) **20.** (a)

21. (a) **22.** (b) **23.** (d) **24.** (c) **25.** (d) **26.** (c) **27.** (c) **28.** (b) **29.** (b) **30.** (c)

31. (c) **32.** (b) **33.** (d) **34.** (a) **35.** (b)